Delegating with Confidence

Jonathan Coates and Claire Breeze

Dr Jonathan Coates was educated as a scientist and an engineer. He worked in the oil industry before becoming involved with management development. Prior to establishing his own company, Jonathan Coates & Associates, he was director of training for the TSB Group. He is the author of a number of books on management.

Claire Breeze is a qualified counsellor and stress adviser, with an M.Sc. in Change Agent Skills and Strategies from the University of Surrey. She is currently leading a number of action learning sets, including one in London for senior women managers. As a consultant she specialises in developing internal consultancy skills.

Jonathan Coates and Claire Breeze are the directors of the Centre for Action Learning Ltd (CALL).

TRAINING EXTRAS is a comprehensive series covering all the crucial management skill areas. Each booklet includes the key issues, helpful starting points and practical advice in a concise and lively style. Together, they form an accessible library reflecting current best practice – ideal for study or quick reference.

Other titles in the series include:

The Appraisal Discussion Terry Gillen

Asking Questions Ian MacKay

Businesslike Budgeting Eric Parsloe and Raymond Wright

Constructive Feedback Roland and Frances Bee

Customer Care Frances and Roland Bee

The Disciplinary Interview Alan Fowler

Effective Learning Alan Mumford

Listening Skills Ian MacKay

Making Meetings Work Patrick Forsyth

The Manager as Coach and Mentor Eric Parsloe

Managing Your Time Iain Maitland

Motivating People Iain Maitland

Negotiating, Persuading and Influencing Alan Fowler

The Selection Interview Penny Hackett

Working in Teams Alison Hardingham

The Institute of Personnel and Development is the leading publisher of books and reports for personnel and training professionals and students and for all those concerned with the effective management and development of people at work. For full details of all our titles please telephone the Publishing Department on 0181 263 3387.

Delegating with Confidence

Jonathan Coates and Claire Breeze

INSTITUTE OF PERSONNEL AND DEVELOPMENT

© Jonathan Coates and Claire Breeze 1996

First published in 1996

All rights reserved. No part of this publication may be reproduced, stored in a retrieval system, or transmitted in any form or by any means, electronic, mechanical, photocopying, recording or otherwise, without written permission of the Institute of Personnel and Development, IPD House, Camp Road, London SW19 4UX.

Design and typesetting by Paperweight
Printed in Great Britain by
Short Run Press, Exeter

British Library Cataloguing in Publication Data
A catalogue record for this book is available from the British Library

ISBN
0-85292-649-9

The views expressed in this book are the authors' own and may not necessarily reflect those of the IPD.

**INSTITUTE OF PERSONNEL
AND DEVELOPMENT**

IPD House, Camp Road, London SW19 4UX
Tel.: 0181 971 9000   Fax: 0181 263 3333
Registered office as above. Registered Charity No. 1038333.
A company limited by guarantee. Registered in England No. 2931892.

Contents

Chapter 1	**What Do We Mean by Delegation?**	1
Chapter 2	**The Basic Process**	6
Chapter 3	**The Difference between Theory and Practice**	22
Chapter 4	**Delegation as a Way of Helping People to Learn**	29
Chapter 5	**Delegation: Being on the Receiving End**	32
Further Reading		35

1
What Do We Mean by Delegation?

When delegation works successfully two things happen simultaneously. First, your staff members take charge of some of your work, which develops their ability and potential. Secondly, this allows you time and space to do the most important parts of your job really well.

Delegation is a complex process which, like other management activities, has to be carefully planned and monitored. It is not simply a question of saying 'I'm too busy to do this, you do it', or 'I don't feel like doing this, you take it on.' This is called 'dumping' and the fact that it begins with a 'd' is the end of its connection with delegation.

Delegation is not something that helps only you; it also gives your staff scope to develop themselves. It will add to your confidence and theirs. In this book we start off by looking at the various planning steps that need to be considered before you start, and at the way in which you build delegation into normal line management. We include some exercises which you can carry out to turn the basic broad ideas into precise business plans. We also look at some of the reasons why this process frequently doesn't work as well as it could. It is common sense to delegate but many people don't do it, or do it badly.

Some reasons why it gives difficulties
Managing other people who are doing 'your' work

People are often highly trained for the work they do. They may have been formally trained in a university or have a formal qualification such as an accountancy diploma or an NVQ; or they may have done it all by hard work and experience. Naturally they are proud of the way they have achieved their expertise and they believe that their way of doing the work is the correct way.

Delegation requires managers not to do the work themselves but to supervise or manage other people who do it. It is hardly surprising that they feel nervous about this process.

They ask:

- will their colleagues be able to carry it out at all?
- will their colleagues be able to carry it out to their standards?

Hands off!

It is hardly surprising that people are nervous about delegation and will frequently say 'It's quicker to do it myself', or 'It takes so long to show them I could have done it in half the time.'

Like all change, it needs investment of time and effort in the short term to pay dividends in the medium to long term. This is always a dilemma for busy people who tend to work in the 'here and now' with the bottom line nagging them for performance and results. They often say 'How can I stop doing what I'm doing really well with absolutely no slack in the system, to train somebody else who may not be able to do it as well as I can?' It is certainly risky and it involves certain guesses; it is not guaranteed and it may not work – but then, what will?

Delegation is not about abandoning your work. We ask the question 'If I am delegating as much as I can, what will I do myself?' We discuss this later because it is a vital issue. It is about change, and moving into areas where you may never have been before, but into which your job is forcing you to develop. It may be comforting not to delegate but to hang on to the things you do well so that you don't have to face up to the challenge of change, leadership and innovation.

The advantages of delegating

- It saves you time to do important things well.
- It increases the capabilities and competencies of your staff members.
- It gives enormous pleasure and pride as more people get seriously involved with your work.
- It provides flexibility to organise your work knowing that you have alternative resources.
- It allows you to concentrate on more difficult and important things.
- It allows you to think, research, discuss, and develop for the future.

In short, it makes you a real manager.

The disadvantages of delegating

- I want it done my way, and my way is the only way.
- I need to control everything.
- It takes time and it may not work.
- If I train them and supervise them and delegate my work to them they will get promoted and move on.
- Eventually they may take my job.

Question: 'When are people ready to be delegated to?' Answer (trick answer to trick question): 'Never!' (Think about it.)

What's in it for me?

Achieving successful delegation is a key step in your development as a real manager. The ability to manage other people doing the work you used to do yourself, and keeping your hands off, is a cornerstone of your own development. Look at the hierarchy of management in your organisation. At the bottom end of the scale, the first line managers, or supervisors, continue to do much of the work themselves and may delegate only some of it. Look at the role of chief executives of large organisations. They simply cannot do any of the hands-on work themselves because there is far too much to do and they may not be expert in it. To move up the management hierarchy you have to understand, and be skilled in, delegating work and managing those who do it. You may eventually manage people who will in turn delegate work to others, and you will need to manage their delegation. You can't manage their delegation unless you know how to do it yourself and put it into practice in an effective way.

So delegating successfully is an important skill and competence for you to acquire.

- It gives you more time to concentrate on important things such as change and innovation.
- It gives you the satisfaction of seeing your team develop.
- It adds to the resources of your unit and will increase its effectiveness and output.

Delegation is not a risk-free process; it will require patience and encouragement. People will make mistakes and they will need to know what will happen when they make a mistake as a result of inexperience.

Some years ago in the United States Home Department – the equivalent of the Home Office in the UK – we saw an active campaign called 'Prove that your boss's job isn't necessary.' This was an official, not an underground, campaign and all around the organisation people were going to their bosses saying 'Let me do that', 'I can do that.' This was quite stimulating and healthy. People were taking work off their bosses' desks; work which they were perfectly capable of doing. It pulled the work downwards, leaving experienced people free to do experienced things. We have to say it also led to one or two people being completely caught out, as they had surrounded themselves with years and years of trivia which they pretended was highly-paid executive work.

What's in it for them?

This is an important question because from your position in your organisation you may see the advantages to yourself and to the organisation, but you have to make sure that your staff members see advantages in it too.

Later in this book we talk about the conflict between job descriptions and delegation, and ask the question 'Whose job is it, anyway?' You may encounter resistance at first, as people conclude that what you are doing is simply making their workload heavier while yours gets lighter. It is important, therefore, that you offer benefits to your staff. It will enlarge their jobs and increase their capacity; it offers more responsibility and more self-development; it really is an opportunity.

It is also important that if you are delegating to staff who are at very low levels in the organisation, and therefore have no one to whom they can delegate, that you don't turn them into a group of 'put-upons' or the organisation's dustbin. The distinction between delegation and dumping has to be handled very carefully at this level. One of the consequences of this may be that delegating at the lower end of an organisation may be more time consuming, because of their suspicion, than it might be at higher levels.

Many of the benefits of successful delegation lie in the medium to long term. That is to say anything from a year to five years. The short term may be difficult and disruptive for you and your staff. People have to learn new skills and competencies. They have to learn to change. This may take them away from what they like doing, and are used to doing, to things you require of them in the future. Don't rush this part of the process; take plenty of time to explain why the change is beneficial for everyone. Don't hesitate to keep talking, not only about the tasks you are delegating but about the value of the whole process.

You may, of course, fail to motivate and persuade someone who is perfectly capable of taking on a delegated task. This is discouraging, but nothing is guaranteed to be successful in management.

Conclusion

In a short book about time management that we wrote some years ago we said 'delegate everything you can'. People frequently challenge us on this because they don't believe it is possible. For instance, they say 'I have no staff', or 'My staff are already overburdened.' The truth in these cases is that you can't delegate, simply because you have not got the necessary resources. But if it is possible and you do have the resources, then delegate as much as possible and make it known that this is your policy. Furthermore, make it known to those taking responsibility for delegated tasks that they too should delegate everything that they can to their staff.

In this way organisations change from being focused on the everyday routine tasks to becoming more managerial, and eventually more strategic. By becoming strategic you learn to make change, innovation and creative thinking your normal way of working, and not just an occasional way that disrupts the *status quo* or the daily work.

We have called this book *Delegating with Confidence* as we know that many people see the common sense of delegation but fear the consequences so much that they don't do it. Confidence comes from following the steps that we set out in the next chapter, and from being aware of the fact that what may seem obvious to you may not be so to your staff.

Authors' note: We have looked for appropriate names to call the people involved in delegation. We did not like delegator/delegatee and although the idea of the word 'delegate', like a Roman soldier, was interesting it is not really common English. Gerard Egan uses 'Manager and Associate', which has some appeal. We didn't like 'subordinate' either.
So finally we have decided to use 'manager and staff member'.

2

The Basic Process

It will be clear from some of the ideas sketched out in the first chapter that delegation is not a hasty and reactive process but needs careful planning and careful implementation. In this chapter we look at the basic steps you have to take in order to delegate confidently. We include a number of practical exercises to help you turn vague thoughts into management reality.

Our experience tells us that people would delegate better if they had a simple action plan and worked through it against an agreed time-scale, rather than suddenly realising in a panic that they shouldn't be doing something – if only somebody else could do it for them! This is common, but at the very moment when you wish somebody else could do it, it is usually too late to delegate or even dump it because you will almost certainly have a deadline that is staring you in the face.

The 10 basic steps of delegating with confidence:
1. what can you delegate?
2. to whom can you delegate it?
3. how much of it will you delegate?
4. how much learning and supervision will be needed?
5. how to motivate staff to do the task
6. doing the supervision and helping the learning
7. setting up a control system
8. handing over the task
9. telling people what you have done, and who is now responsible for the task
10. making delegation a normal part of management practice.

If you look at this list carefully you will see that this is similar to the recruitment and selection process:

- what is the job?
- who would be the ideal person?
- how will they learn and be supervised?
- how and when will they be left to get on with it?

There are many parallels between careful planning for delegation and recruiting a new employee.

Step 1 What can you delegate?

List all the tasks you currently perform. Thinking about the following might help:

- your whole working day, week, month, year
- your objectives
- problems that crop up all the time
- how you use your time and where the time pressures are
- your interaction with customers
- the way you work with your boss.

You may have listed 20 or 30 items. Examples of tasks might be:

- preparing quarterly reports
- research and implement IT networking
- introducing ISO 9000
- organise press conference
- maintenance of X or Y machine
- advertising for office cleaners.

Exercise 1 What to delegate

Make yourself a table as outlined in Figure 2.1 on page 8. In Column 1 write down your list of tasks. For each task ask yourself some questions and tick the appropriate column relating to your response.

8   Delegating with Confidence

Figure 2.1

1	2	3	4	5	6
TASK	I must do this myself	Vital tasks that must be done correctly	I like doing this	Why should anybody do this?	Tasks I can delegate

Column 2 I must do this myself

There are certainly some tasks you will have to do yourself and this may be for legal or statutory reasons so it is impossible to delegate them. Remember that although you may be legally responsible for carrying out certain tasks you don't necessarily have to do the actual work yourself.

We once had a heated argument with a senior customs officer who insisted that it was his job to check the whisky levels in all the vats at the distillery. This involved days of clambering around dusty warehouses. In truth he was legally obliged only to ensure the job was done properly, without doing the dipping and testing himself. We suspect he rather liked it!

Column 3 Vital tasks that must be done correctly

In theory we would like to get everything right, but the reality is that people are required to do more and more with fewer resources. You must therefore make choices about those things that have to be done very well indeed, with the consequence that other things will be done in a rather less than perfect way and may even be skimmed over.

Identifying the important tasks is crucial but it does not mean you have to do them yourself. Delegating them to somebody else, with careful supervision, might be possible.

Column 4 I like doing this

This is a common barrier to delegation. You tend to cling to tasks which really have little importance but are ones you feel comfortable with or like doing. In the Video Arts film, *The Unorganised Manager*, St Peter calls this 'growing up'.

Column 5 Why should anybody do this?

Organisations drift and change, and tasks which were important two years ago may have very little value now. It is not a question of delegating; it is a question of stopping doing them. The monthly meeting – important during the change of office project – has become redundant. Don't delegate chairing the meeting to somebody else – scrap it!

Column 6 Tasks I can delegate

Put a tick in this column where there are tasks you should delegate totally or partially.

Exercise 2 Things we should be doing but are not

One way of delegating is to ask yourself 'Why am I doing this when somebody else could be doing it?' or 'What am I not doing that is important, or failing to do well; things that if I gave myself space and time I could give proper attention to?' This exercise tweaks your conscience.

Figure 2.2 What I ought to be doing

Tasks I am not doing well enough or at all	New tasks	More effort/time required
Developing a marketing strategy		
	Visiting all subsidiary companies (UK)	
		Giving more time and effort to communicate impending changes

- Draw up a table as in Figure 2.2. Look at your table from Exercise 1 and find the things you are not doing well enough, if at all. Write these in Column 1.
- In Column 2 you should indicate whether they are new tasks.
- In Column 3 you should indicate whether more effort or quality time is needed.

The point of these two exercises is to make you think carefully about your job and the things you could delegate, in order to concentrate on the important things you must do yourself. Derek Rayner, later Lord Rayner, who made such sweeping changes in the organisation of the Civil Service after his success at Marks & Spencer plc, said '... for me what makes a good manager is someone who can find large chunks of time to do important things properly'. We all recognise the truth here.

Step 2 To whom can you delegate it?

You should now have a list of tasks that you would like to delegate. Against this list you should match the staff to whom you might delegate certain tasks. We have to be careful here. How much do you want to delegate? Some books talk about delegation as if it were like turning on a light – it is either on or off. You delegate to A or you do it yourself. In truth this limits the possibilities of delegation. We see the process as more like a light with a dimmer switch where you can adjust the level of light through varying degrees, depending on the need. Figure 2.3 will explain this more clearly.

Figure 2.3 Levels of delegation

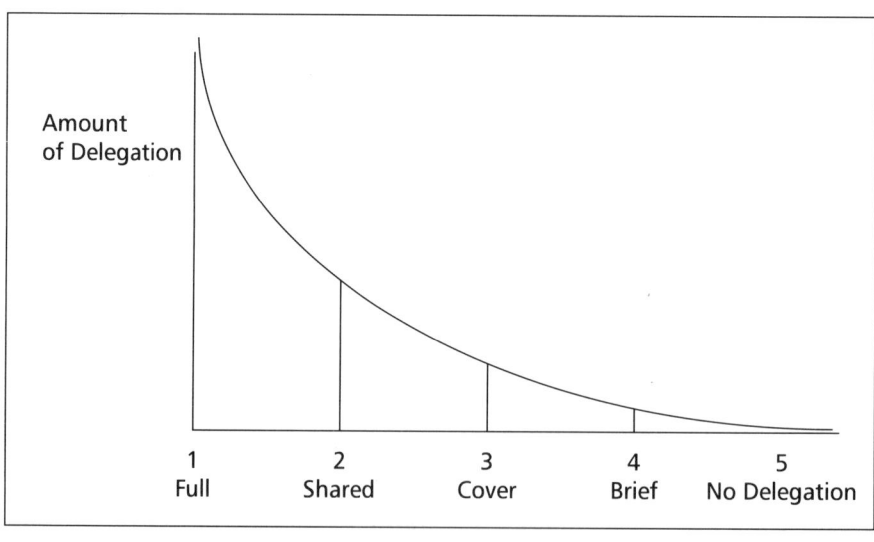

Stage 1   Full delegation:
            Your staff member takes over the task fully.
Stage 2   Shared delegation:
            You and your staff member share the task and agree who will be responsible for which parts. This is useful when the person is not

ready to take full responsibility but can do elements of it now whilst learning others later.

Stage 3 'Cover in my absence' delegation:
At this stage the staff member is ready to take over enough of the task to keep things moving when you are away.

Stage 4 'Brief every time' delegation:
At this stage the staff member is not ready to take on a large part of the task but may contribute usefully each time the task occurs, while needing to be reminded of details and instructions.

Stage 5 No delegation:
You keep all the task to yourself.

The purpose of this exercise is to allow you to get the maximum flexibility out of delegating. If you can only work at Stage 1, giving full responsibility to the staff member, some of the other possibilities available to you are lost. On the other hand, depending on how much of the task you want to delegate, you may have to provide more training and supervision.

Step 3 How much of it will you delegate?

Exercise 3 How much work will it involve me in?

Draw up a table like Figure 2.4.

This table is for two people, John and Mary; and for only two tasks: prepare the monthly report and advertise for cleaners. In reality there will be more tasks and more staff members. The tasks will be taken from Exercises 1 and 2.

Figure 2.4

TASK	JOHN Level of delegation	JOHN Amount of training	JOHN Amount of supervision	MARY Level of delegation	MARY Amount of training	MARY Amount of supervision
Task 1 eg monthly report	2	Medium	Medium			
Task 2 eg advertise for cleaners				4	Low	Medium

Step 4 How much learning and supervision will be needed?

Look carefully at each task and the person to whom that you plan to delegate it. Think about the level of delegation (on a scale from 1 to 4 from Figure 2.3). Generally speaking, the more delegation you propose the more training and supervision will be needed. We suggest you designate the amount of training and supervision as High, Medium or Low.

Our example shows that if you delegate Task 1 to John as shared delegation (level 2) then in your view he will need a medium level of training and a medium level of supervision. On the other hand, if you delegate Task 2 to Mary at level 4 (brief her again on what you want her to do) then you need only a low level of training but still a medium level of supervision.

Most people delegate by the seat of their pants. They simply decide they do not want to or cannot do the task any more, and dump it on a colleague. This exercise allows you to look at each task and at each staff member, matching abilities to tasks. There is no point in planning to delegate everything at once and then getting lost in a deluge of training and supervision.

Once you have completed the table as fully as you can you will know what is possible, but so far you have made no decisions. What would be a reasonable time to devote to the process of delegating these tasks? Will you have to train the staff yourself or will it involve the training department? Are you still sure you want to delegate to the degree you have decided? Go over your table as many times as you need, revising your decisions until you have a clear picture of your resulting workload if these tasks were to be delegated as you have outlined. Now you have a plan of what you will delegate and what it will involve.

Step 5 How to motivate staff to do the task

The argument so far has been to make a case for delegation. After all the work you have done the advantages of delegation will be clear. It is not enough that the people to whom you wish to delegate are capable and have some spare capacity; they also have to want to do it. Without the motivation to do the work you are offering them, the delegation will fail. So why should they be as interested as you are in taking on what appears to be more work and quite possibly more difficult work?

Of course, some staff will naturally enjoy the challenge and the potential that delegated work offers them to stretch their abilities. They will see it as an opportunity to extend themselves and develop a higher profile whilst becoming more competent and effective. There is no question that there are people like this in most organisations and they are keen to do as much as they can, partly for self-satisfaction and partly to be seen and valued by the organisation.

Equally, there are some who may not see your approach quite so positively. They may interpret your actions as an attempt to get them to do, without pay, what they regard as your job. Don't be surprised if people say '…that is your job; it's in your job description and that's what you're paid to do. I'm not interested in doing any of that.' It may be that one way to encourage them to support you is to ask for their help. 'It would be a great help to me if….', or 'It would help the department if we could arrange things in a different way…' This is not grovelling; it is positive.

Another approach might be to build on the things they can call their own. Instead of being asked to do routine tasks, they might want to adopt a task and be in charge of it. For instance, they might be in charge of day-to-day accounts, or targeting the submanagers in the field. This implies (and it is important) that delegation is not simply about passing on the routine tasks that nobody else wants. It is inevitable that low-level tasks are an everyday part of any organisation, but staff get bored or resentful if they feel they have more than their fair share of them. You should try to share these out as well as the more meaningful, high-profile tasks.

Another approach would be to see if you could appeal to their sense of improvement and achievement. Be careful that you don't frustrate yourself, and your staff too, by wondering why they aren't more like you – at their age and position you would have given anything for someone to offer you more responsibility. But they are not like you and there is no reason why they should be. We discuss this idea more fully in Chapter 4 when we look at the connection between delegation and learning.

Another form of resistance that they may produce is '… I am quite happy with the way things are … especially if you're not offering me more money for doing more work'. It is not easy for people to give up a situation with which they are familiar and comfortable, even though they can see the advantages of moving forward. Communicating your ideas may take much longer than you thought would be necessary. You will have to communicate the proposed changes again and again before your staff are willing to adopt something which seems obvious to you.

Saying 'yes' and meaning it

You need to persuade people to take on new responsibilities. How will you know whether they have really agreed to it or not? What will agreement look like? Of course they will say 'yes' – in organisations it is generally advisable! There is a big difference between people saying yes and meaning it. What would you really expect to happen that would demonstrate their commitment to taking on this piece of work?

You might ask them gently but firmly to think through the implications of not doing it; of staying where they are, and not just for the next few weeks. The implications of not moving with the organisation can be a powerful force to make people think about adopting something they hadn't done before. Make sure they are aware that training and support will be available until they are completely ready. Make sure they understand that they won't be abandoned in the deep end. Let them think through the implications of not taking on the task, and leave them to think it through before responding.

Step 6 Doing the supervision and helping the learning

Now all the parts are in place – you can begin delegating.

You have chosen the tasks, the staff, and the degree to which you want to delegate. You have thought about the person to whom you will delegate, and why they might be motivated to do it. You have made a plan looking at the supervision and the amount of learning needed to reach the appropriate level of delegation. Now you can move on to the next step.

Training and training plans

It is important to remember that you are not training people that you are going to despatch to operate independently in another part of the world. They will be with you and you can help them. You don't need to over-train them or be too rigorous in your approach to a training plan.

In the Second World War an American called Flanagan was given responsibility for training Spitfire pilots. He would have liked at least six weeks with each new pilot, but he was given just three days. Therefore he had to select, from all the things he would have *liked* to teach, the things he *had* to teach. This became known as Flanagan's Law of Criticality. What are the critical things that people have to get right in the task to be delegated?

It is very important that part of the motivation contains an answer to the question 'Why are we doing this?' You should listen to their view, their ideas and involvement in the way they learn the task. It may be that seen through a fresh pair of eyes the task may be improved or simplified. You may find that you have become so used to doing it one way you have not thought about an alternative method.

Delegation involves two people and should be regarded as a teamwork exercise that can add value. Please give it enough time. All change is time-consuming. Don't rush things and don't expect them to be able to do it overnight.

Remember also that your approach to some of these tasks has probably become automatic because they are familiar to you. If you watch an expert doing something expertly, the chances are that they are not thinking about what they are doing. So when you stall your car, you don't go through all the steps in the manual; you simply get it going and rejoin the traffic. Look at your own approach to some of your tasks and see if you can work out which things you have learned that you didn't know at first; what it feels like when it's going well and, more importantly, how you can pass on this knowledge to someone else.

You may find there are other useful ways of helping the learning process. Can your training department provide help? Are there similar activities in other departments to which your staff member can go and observe? Can they begin to represent you right now by taking part in meetings on your behalf? In Chapter 4 we will again look at delegation as a learning opportunity.

These ideas will help you to construct a training plan which should simply be a calendar of parts of the task assigned to certain dates. Experience shows that most delegated tasks need to be divided into no more than six or eight subtasks, and often less. Think about the subtasks, discuss them with the staff member concerned, and then write down all the things they need to know and how they are going to learn them.

You will also need a method of finding out the rate at which the learning is taking place. It is not sufficient to get to the end of it all and then find out that there are still problems. Regular assessment will help you put things right if they're going wrong.

Praise, encouragement and giving feedback

Someone once said that the thing that makes a great teacher is a good knowledge of the subject (but not necessarily the best in the world) and the ability to encourage. As delegating managers we are here to do just that – be an expert in our subject and encourage others to become expert.

What is the difference between praise and encouragement? Praise is nearly always used when something has been completed successfully. (It would be unusual for someone to be praised when something has gone wrong.) Encouragement is used when things go well or badly, and may not always be kept until the job is complete.

We suggest that in order to understand more fully the process of giving feedback you should read *Constructive Feedback* by Roland and Frances Bee (London, IPD, 1996).

Admitting that things may go wrong is part of the learning and supervising process. Things *will* go wrong. People will not always get things right first time. Is it clear what your attitude will be when someone makes a mistake – even a fairly major one? Will you snatch back the delegated task or adopt an attitude of ridicule and sarcasm, or will you ask them to take you through the process to the point of the mistake and discuss why you regard it as a mistake? We hope it is obvious to you which of these approaches you should take.

Supervision

Delegation can be exasperating when mistakes are made, especially when you are trying to get results out of people in areas where you can do it competently yourself. This is not a charter for wantonness; irresponsible and reckless behaviour is not what we are talking about. We are talking here about genuine mistakes made by people getting into difficulties whilst learning.

One of the things you need to establish is which things have to be done in a particular way, and which ones can be changed to suit the style of the person taking on the task. There are some things where you can leave them to work out the best way of doing it, while there are others where you have to be absolutely strict and unequivocal about the degree of flexibility.

Establishing priorities carefully and checking them regularly is part of supervision. Try to encourage your staff member to challenge you when you give woolly instructions in terms of time or priority. If this challenge can be seen as professional and helpful, rather than impertinent, your relationship will flourish.

Step 7 Setting up a control system

In a recent project in Ghana we asked the managers on the programme to go between courses to enquire how much delegated work was properly controlled. One enquirer came back to suggest that out of 20 delegated tasks only one had been controlled or followed through to ensure it was being done successfully. Delegation is about increasing the resources of the organisation, to increase its capacity, not about abandoning work to junior members of staff because we have no further interest in it. This story gives a frightening picture of an organisation not under control.

There is a famous law which is very short and is attributed to many authors. It is sometimes known as Murphy's Law or Sod's Law. It says quite simply, 'If things can go wrong, they will.' Things go wrong for you and, therefore, will go wrong for staff to whom you have delegated work. This will be especially true in the early days of delegating, when staff are relatively inexperienced. However keen and intelligent they may be, you may find things go wrong and that they may be unaware of it.

Part of delegation is to establish some control systems which allow the manager and staff member to know how they will keep in touch with each other. This is not checking up, especially if it is built into the process early on. It will look more like checking up if it is done on a random or hasty basis.

Establishing control is not the same thing as interfering. When you delegate you have to step back and let staff members learn to do it in their own way and at their own pace. Only recently we talked with a very senior, and very exasperated, civil servant. 'In theory they delegate all this to me and then they want to do everything themselves, especially the trivial bits.'

Control means establishing in advance a regular method of giving feedback on what is happening. At the beginning this is done over quite short time spans; once delegation is more established the time span gets longer.

Examples of controls could be:

- reports – summaries not wordy documents
- meetings – specially set up to discuss progress; short term – daily lasting 15 minutes; long term – weekly or even monthly meetings.

Other kinds of checkpoints for making contact and feeding back within delegation could be:

- the first time that something is completed
- when someone has made their first field trip
- when 90 per cent of the budget is spent
- when we have been to 16 out of 20 branches.

The important thing is to ensure that feedback is given in sufficient time to enable both parties to spot things that are going wrong, on a time-scale that still allows the original outcome to be achieved. It would be foolish to put in a checkpoint at the very last minute when, if something has gone wrong, it is too late to do anything about it.

Step 8 Handing over the task

When the preparation, training and supervision are complete you can both celebrate. It would be a real culture shock if organisations regularly celebrated the successful conclusion of a delegated task!

However, the story is not quite over and we have a few more details to put into place. The golden rule of delegating is that the manager who is delegating the task remains responsible for its achievement. This is a crucial statement in the process of delegation, and it worries many people. They say 'Now I've put all this effort into preparing somebody to take over a task in a delegated way, why do I have to retain the responsibility for it?' Well, it is your responsibility because it is in *your* list of things to achieve. The fact that somebody else will be doing most of the work doesn't change your overall responsibility. If mistakes are made and the staff member fails to deliver whatever is required of them, you can be cross, angry, patient or understanding but you continue to be responsible to the organisation for having failed to meet the deadline or achieve the task. And when they perform really well you should give lots of credit both publicly and privately. It may have needed real effort and tenacity to do the work to the right standard. You may be able to reward it in some small but valued way. Tell the world proudly what your staff member has achieved.

However, as well as the particular delegated job, you do hand over a number of things to your staff as part of the delegating process; these are concerned with authority, accountability and agreed control systems and checkpoints.

Authority

Many problems within organisations arise from people being given delegated tasks without the full authority to carry them out. They feel hamstrung and held back when they are constantly having to say 'I think we can go ahead with this but I am going to have to ask first.' This is because their authority has not been fully established at the point where the delegation process is complete. Research shows that this lack of authority is one of the leading causes of stress within organisations. Authority defines exactly what the staff member can do or decide without consultation. This could be that you can take all the decisions on recruitment and selection of branch staff. That is a clear statement of where you have the authority to act and, by implication, where you don't have authority to act. So you would clearly be able to recruit all branch staff from managers to clerks but you have no authority to recruit head office staff or regional office staff.

Accountability

Accountability is defined by authority, so if you exceed your authority you will be accountable for your actions. You have the authority to say how long a project will take so long as it is within a certain limit. If it takes longer than that, someone will want to know why. If you have £100,000 to spend on transport and you spend £130,000 then your boss will want to know why.

Learning from experience

Delegating important tasks to your staff is a key part of their development. It gives them the opportunity to do new things and to develop themselves and learn. It also allows that things might go wrong. The fact that things go wrong does not always entail blame and penalty. Similarly, in learning about management we can apply the same sort of questions when things have not gone exactly the way we should have foreseen. There are three important questions:

- What did we set out to do and what actually happened?
- What can we learn from this?
- What will we do next time?

It is by accepting accountability and authority that people learn how they can operate, and to what limits. This gives a framework for finding out what has been learned and what has not.

An important step in delegation is defining exactly what has been delegated and what level of authority and accountability is appropriate. It may be that when you start delegating you have some ideas about what these levels might be, but they change in the course of the learning and supervision. Perhaps you realise that you can delegate more to this individual and with more authority than you had originally intended. Maybe you realise that although the person is able to be delegated to, they may have to wait before they can take full authority and accountability for the task.

This is a form of contracting between individuals. It defines what they can and cannot do. It defines what success will look like. It might, depending on your organisational procedures, include what people get paid. This kind of contract could well be written down and become part of the way in which work is defined in your objective-setting system. Writing it down makes it an agreement according to which both parties are obliged to work.

Step 9 Telling people what you have done, and who is now responsible for the task

One of the most curious things about delegation is that people forget to tell everyone else in the organisation what has happened. When you have completed all the stages of delegation, you must tell everyone about the new circumstances. You make an announcement – 'As from 1 July Angela Smith is in charge of all our accounting procedures. Please send her with the following reports …'

The obvious intention of this is that people will go direct to Angela with their data and their questions. They will leave you alone, allowing you the time and space to do other things. Despite the obvious benefits of this, people often don't make the announcement. They fail to do so for a number of reasons. First, they are worried about being seen to give away some of their own power and authority. Secondly, we know that although delegation appears to be encouraged, many organisations are ambivalent about it. This causes some managers who delegate properly to feel ashamed – they feel they will be perceived as letting go of things they ought to keep for themselves.

We would suggest that the announcement should be made in writing and that people are formally told that Angela Smith, who has been taken through a proper process of delegation and training, is now responsible for the work to this degree of authority.

Step 10 Making delegation a normal part of management practice

After all the steps in delegating, which may take a short or long time depending on how big the task is, it is time to incorporate the changes into a regular way of working. There may need to be adjustments to job descriptions and annual objectives. This may lead to conflict with the existing job description. What you are asking your staff member to do may not be in their job description and this is a sensitive issue which may need to be handled carefully. You have changed their job, and they have changed and grown into a larger job. It is unlikely that at this stage, having gone through all the steps, they will object to what you have done but it is just possible that they may comment, even at this late stage, that their job differs from their job description. This is the way that organisations and people develop and there is no need for you to be defensive about it.

Having incorporated the changes into the job description you now need to set performance objectives on your normal six- or twelve-month cycle and use these objectives as a dynamic way of measuring performance. The good supervision, helping, encouraging and controlling practice you developed for delegation does not stop once the person is doing the job in their own way.

And what about you?

Now you have delegated these tasks what are you going to do? What are you going to move on to now that you have given yourself more space and time? Go back to the exercises and the tables at the beginning of this chapter to see what it is you should now be doing. The development of staff through delegation is one of the key components of the manager's job. But it is not only for their benefit, but for that of the manager also.

3
The Difference between Theory and Practice

Most of us know that there can be a difference between theory and practice when it comes to delegating. The plans you make on training courses, and the good intentions you may have after reading the first chapters of this book, can soon fall by the wayside.

In our experience of working with managers we have found that they often construct some apparently plausible reasons for not delegating. These become so ingrained into the way that they work, it is hard to realise that some of them were simply excuses in the first place. In this chapter we are going to look at the most common reasons that managers give for not delegating to their staff.

Let us start with a simple exercise. Look down the list below and see how many of these reasons you have used in order to avoid delegating. You will get the most out of this exercise if you are frank with yourself. Remember that most of us have used these reasons at some time in our careers, so don't be worried that you are a 'bad' manager just because you have reasoned in this way. All of these statements have been collected from managers that we have worked with over the past eight years.

Reasons for not delegating to my staff

- **Speed**
  'I can do it more quickly than they can.'
  'By the time I've explained it, I could have done it myself.'

- **Accuracy**
  'They won't do it exactly the way I want it.'
  'They are bound to make mistakes and I'll only end up correcting it.'

- **Preference**
  'I quite like doing this myself.'
  'It is too important for anyone but me to be doing.'

- **Fear**
  'They may do it better than me.'
  'I won't know what is going on any more.'

Speed

The speed with which delegated work is done is often a cause for concern to managers. Most of us are busier these days and are required to produce more with fewer resources, or so it seems. In delegation there are two main issues to do with speed that can block us from doing what we know is effective management practice.

The first hurdle is the belief that the time it will take us to pass over the piece of work and ensure that our staff member understands what the work is about, could be used for simply getting on with it ourselves. Of course, this is an accurate belief and it would be hard to disagree with, except, that is, in the long term. We once worked with a senior manager who told us that she did not have the time to delegate a particular piece of work to a member of her staff as it was taking her five hours a week to complete, and she simply couldn't find the time to pass it on! In the short-term view of her working week, this was a difficult argument to fault. However, each week she found herself spending all that time on an activity that she could well have delegated. Eventually she had to learn a simple but hard lesson, that she needed to invest more time during the first few weeks as she delegated effectively, in order to buy back five hours every week for the foreseeable future.

Our short-term approach to managing often limits the effective choices we can make as a future investment. If you are in this position, now is the time to calculate how much of your time would be needed over the next few weeks to delegate a task effectively, and compare this with how much time you will accumulate for other tasks. We are confident that when you analyse it you will find the exchange worthwhile.

The second hurdle concerning speed often comes after we have made the commitment to delegate a piece of work, and have started to do so. When you are familiar with a piece of work you are likely to handle it relatively quickly and with a degree of competence. Members of your staff who are not so familiar with the work will naturally need more time to complete it, and in some cases may never be as quick as you are. It is important to the delegation process that you take this transitional period into account, particularly in setting time limits which meet a genuine organisational requirement rather than just your own personal preference.

Taking Action

- Analyse the time that a particular task is regularly taking and compare this with the time you will need to allocate to delegating the task to someone else.
- Draw up a list of other more important activities that you could undertake if you delegate this task.
- In the early stages of the delegation process, set time-scales that reflect the familiarity of the task to the person concerned.
- Check that your proposed deadlines really are what the organisation requires, not simply your personal time-scales.

Accuracy

The hurdles to do with accuracy are also of two types. First there is the management thinking process that requires members of our staff to produce work 'in our image', so that although we are delegating the work to them we are really expecting it to be done exactly as we would do it. The second hurdle is often more difficult for managers, because it concerns mistakes.

People work in different ways, often to produce the same outputs. This can be a matter of personal style and experience. You should be concerned only where there is a sound organisational requirement for work to be done in one particular way. These reasons may include legal requirements, strategic expectations or cultural norms. Other reasons often stem from our own tried and tested methods or simply because we believe that our way is the best.

It is important to apply some managerial common sense to this problem when you are planning to delegate a piece of work to a member of your staff. Try to separate out issues to do with the work that are mandatory and therefore fixed, from other areas where it is possible for them to apply their own creativity to the work in order to make it their own.

Making mistakes, or simply the anxiety that they may occur after delegation, can form a very solid block to initiating the process effectively. We once worked with a company that claimed as part of its mission statement 'We make no mistakes.' It is easy to appreciate the sentiment behind the statement as praiseworthy, but the reality for those people employed by the company was quite different. Mistakes did happen, as they inevitably do, but people spent most of their time covering up their mistakes, blaming others for them and delegating nothing at the managerial level for fear of failure. The net effect of this position was a huge block of work at the managerial level that was never passed down the organisation, and which kept expanding. The result was a group of bored and under-used staff below the managerial tier, with little learning or development across the organisation as a whole. It may not surprise you to learn that this organisation is no longer in business.

Few organisations have a declared policy on mistakes. W H Smith Ltd does have one. This says clearly that making mistakes is part of the way you learn and they should be discussed openly. However, it goes on to say that making the same mistake repeatedly will not be tolerated.

Mistakes happen

Managers should concern themselves with minimising the likelihood of mistakes, but use them, when they do happen, as a tool for developing learning and improving organisational quality. Perfection, or the drive to seek it, is not a bad thing in itself, but it can become such an obsession for managers that they feel compelled to do everything themselves; or worse, they delegate work and then insist on interfering repeatedly or checking even the most insignificant detail. It is the consequences of this approach which are particularly significant in the delegation process, as your staff can become so demotivated that they do not even try to correct their own errors, knowing that you will find them. Thus two people are being paid to do the same job; hardly a recipe for efficiency.

Delegating with confidence demands not only your confidence as the delegating manager, but also that you trust your staff members and openly declare this trust.

Not all mistakes are the same; there are significant mistakes and peripheral mistakes. Identifying potential mistakes within the delegated task before you hand the work over will help you to plan the right level of instruction, and also an appropriate strategy for reacting if things go wrong. Significant mistakes can range from being life-threatening to being extremely costly, while peripheral mistakes may be anything where the damage to your product, reputation or task can be rectified without long-term effects. You will need to exercise your judgement here, and in the early stages of delegating work to others it is important to be prudent without becoming fanatical.

Some mistakes in business are legendary. The story of the Swiss Bank foreign exchange dealer who put the figures in the wrong column and cost his company 100 million dollars is quite well known. We also like the story of the director who made a mistake that cost his company £1 million. At an emergency board meeting called to discuss the crisis he asked the chief executive if he wanted his resignation. 'No,' was the reply. 'We have just invested £1 million in your development and we want a real return on it!'

Taking Action

- As you are planning to delegate, think through what areas of the task *must* be handled in a particular way, and be prepared to explain this.
- Discuss with your staff other possible ways of undertaking the task.
- Identify where the potential mistakes may come and how critical they are.
- Share your ideas with your staff member, and be as specific as possible.
- Plan and direct your help towards these areas particularly.
- Encourage the rapid and open exploration of mistakes with your staff.
- Recall how your own mistakes have been handled by effective managers.

Preference

It comes as no surprise to us that managers spend most of their time, doing what they like to do whenever they can. These activities often bring with them a sense of purpose, value or simple enjoyment. It has often been our experience that managers will happily overcome all of the hurdles to delegate an activity or a task for which they hold no personal preference. Those on the receiving end of delegation can often sense this, and are likely to perceive it as a dumping activity, even if you have tried to follow the good practice laid out in this book. Getting a reputation for shedding those parts of your own work that you do not like will not enhance your capacity to influence your staff in a positive way.

We are not advocating that you shed every part of your job that gives you a particular sense of pleasure merely for the sake of being an effective manager. It is a question of balance and priority. It is not unusual for us to encounter managers who are still hanging on to work that they used to do in their last job simply because they like doing it. This is particularly true where people make the notional transition from specialist work to a managerial role and find it hard to let go. In examples like these, managers are operating from a historical context rather than demonstrating that they are working in a way that reflects where they and the organisation are today.

Comparing your own personal preferences with what the organisation requires of you, will offer you an opportunity to keep up to date with your activities and allow work to flow through the organisation to levels that are appropriate for it. Managers who work only by personal preference are in danger of themselves becoming the block.

Taking Action

- Take a hard look at those pieces of work that you like doing and decide whether they are really appropriate to your current role and priorities.
- Let go of these areas slowly and in a planned way, and replace them with activities that can offer you value for your time.
- Seek out a new activity in line with your current working requirements.
- Start by *sharing* a task with a staff member at first if you are reluctant to let go entirely.

Fear

At the bottom of most of our resistance towards changing ourselves lies some type of fear or anxiety about the consequences. Delegation is no different in this respect. It has been our experience that, for some managers, successfully coping with all the other potential hurdles discussed so far has finally revealed the root of the problem: a fear of what the process might lead to.

For some of us it is a reluctance to accept that others may be more competent or gifted than we are, and that delegating to them will only make this difference more apparent to our colleagues and bosses. For others it can be the sense that delegation implies a lack of control over what is happening, and that our worst fears may be realised. These rather extreme assumptions about what might happen if we delegate to others can be very powerful blocks, even though we may rarely articulate them.

For most of us the hurdles of fear become a self-fulfilling prophecy. If we seek extreme levels of control over the work of others, and refuse to share the more interesting parts of that work with those who are supposed to work for us, we can soon become isolated, resented and bypassed. The majority of people working in organisations want fulfilment and responsibility within their work. We no longer live in a world where managers are automatically respected simply because of their seniority. Being an effective delegator of tasks can be seen as a management competence in its own right. It is a facilitating role that brings with it its own area of expertise and rewards.

Taking Action

- Articulate what is the worst thing that can happen if you delegate a task, establish how likely that is, and build in some checkpoints to prevent it happening.
- Think of the best outcome from delegating this task for you and the staff member.
- Establish which elements of the task you feel that you need more control over, and check these off against your current job function to ascertain whether they are really necessary.
- In discussion with your staff member, establish a mutually acceptable level of control and feedback. Agree to review this frequently to see if it is working. Phase in a reduced level of control linked to each successful outcome from the delegation.
- Ask yourself 'If I have all this control, how does it benefit me?' See if the answers you arrive at are consistent with the management values that you think you hold.

4
Delegation as a Way of Helping People to Learn

There is a connection between delegation and learning which is so integral that we are frequently surprised by the number of managers we meet who have never seen the process of delegation as a learning opportunity, either for themselves or for their staff.

Taking on any new task at work will often require us to learn something new. Sometimes this learning seems to be very significant and quite different from what we are used to; alternatively the type of learning involved may be no more than a subtle shift of emphasis in the way we are currently working. Nevertheless, most delegated tasks will contain an element of learning.

Having read most of this book, you may well feel like testing out some of the ideas by delegating a task to a member of your staff. If this is the case, are you quite confident about your skills in the following areas, as they are the key skills in delegating:

- clarifying objectives
- listening skills
- summarising agreements
- confronting and dealing with broken agreements
- oral encouraging or praising skills
- coaching?

A framework for identifying potential learning

The following broad framework may help you to consider the learning implications of any task that you are delegating. Before you use it on a member of your staff, we suggest that you apply the criteria to your own task of delegating more effectively! Working through these key issues will help you and your staff member to create a 'learning agreement' to achieve the delegated task. The issues fall into four broad categories and can be used to give structure to your joint discussions about learning.

The 4 Rs of a learning agreement
- requirement
- relevance
- routes
- recognition.

Requirement is the amount of learning that the task will require of you, if you are to undertake it as effectively as possible. Requirement is also about the level of the learning that will have to take place in order to perform the task. In some cases the learning may be a significant departure from current practice, in others it may be applying an already well-developed skill in another environment or situation.

Relevance is the degree of connection you can make between the potential learning required for the task and the other areas of work that the person is involved in. Where people can see an added benefit to themselves from learning a new skill, they are more likely to be motivated. Relevance in learning can help to reframe an activity into a positive challenge.

Routes to learning these new skills can be very varied, and need not rely on the traditional training methods that we so often use. There are other ways of learning in the workplace that do not require you to attend courses. You can play a useful role in this area of the delegation process by coaching members of your staff through their tasks in a way that is designed to help them learn. Eric Parsloe has written an excellent book in the Training Extras series entitled *The Manager as Coach and Mentor*; we would recommend it to you if your learning need in the delegation process is to be a more effective coach to your staff. Why not try to identify a learning agreement for yourself from this activity?

Recognition poses a more testing set of questions, as it requires us to be able to demonstrate what we have learned by our actions, not only to ourselves but to those around us. For a manager involved in delegating and coaching, this is an important stage in the process, as it provides you with some firm reassurance that your time and effort have been well spent. These outward indicators form the basis of recognising that delegation is a dual-value process; that is to say that the learner adds value to him or herself and to the organisation. When people have learned to master a newly delegated task the organisation benefits and so do they. If this statement is to have any meaning at all, there must be ways of identifying these benefits from both points of view.

Taking Action

- Always look for the learning potential in a piece of work to be delegated and ensure that this forms part of your dialogue with the person receiving the task.
- Having identified the key elements of learning, agree with the staff member a route towards achieving this learning.
- Brush up your coaching skills before you start so that you can be of maximum help if you are needed.
- Try to find links between the learning that is necessary to the task and any benefits for the person in the rest of their job.
- Identify clearly with the person where you can offer support and what the nature of that support will be. Schedule time to do this.
- Apply these ideas to your own skills in delegating to others. Identify what skills you will need to learn in order to be helpful, and how you can plan a way of learning them. Remember, if the system is useful for your staff it may have some benefits for you too!
- Use the ideas in this chapter to take stock of your own job and find ways of developing it further.

5
Delegation: Being on the Receiving End

Throughout this book we have focused our attention on those of you who are in a position to delegate. However there are two areas that still need addressing if we are to think about delegation from all perspectives. Few of us are in the position where we can delegate to others but are not delegated to ourselves. Most of us sit in a 'delegation sandwich' where we are planning and managing the delegation process to our staff, and are also receiving work from our boss at the same time.

Those who have work delegated to them but who have no one to delegate to have received little attention in the literature; this is the second area. For several years we have worked with groups of people in this position. We have found that they often start by describing their experiences negatively, and feel powerless to do anything about a delegated task which has been given to them with little thought or planning, and rarely with any coaching. This paints a gloomy picture of organisational life, particularly for those of us who experience it on a daily basis.

The delegation sandwich

There is an enormous temptation in organisations to pass on and perpetuate pieces of managerial behaviour that we ourselves have experienced. Even if this is not adopted as a positive strategy, inertia can creep into the way we work. This leads to the stage where we are no longer sensitive to the managerial style we have developed for ourselves. Even those of us who struggle to do right by our organisations and our staff may feel demoralised by receiving inadequately delegated work with little support or encouragement.

Dumping or delegating?

The process of managing upwards in these situations becomes even more critical when you are not in a position yourself to delegate. When the work stops with you, there is little chance of providing a good learning experience for others. The term 'dumping' has become common in the managerial vocabulary and provides us with very negative images of powerless people being showered with work that is poorly defined, not linked to a learning agreement, and inadequately supported. Worse still, it may simply be work that their boss does not want to do!

It is time that those in this position took a more planned approach to receiving delegated work. Our experience of working with groups in this way has shown that both they and the manager who is delegating tasks to them begin to develop a working arrangement that is more satisfying, less stressful and more organisationally effective. Much has been written about empowerment of staff. There are few organisational processes where it is genuinely possible to offer a more empowering opportunity to all levels of staff than through delegation. Breaking out of the cycle of negative experience can be difficult but is not impossible. Over the years we have been at pains to teach those people in this position that it is possible to participate in the process of delegation with your manager, through questioning, clarifying and giving encouraging feedback. Waiting for managers to delegate perfectly could keep us waiting a long time, and simply allow us to build up yet more resentment.

Figure 5.1 Skills for receiving delegation

Stage 1 Getting Clear
- Establish clearly what the task is and what it should look like when it is finished.
- Agree by when the task needs to be completed.
- Clarify what priority the task has in relation to your other work.
- Explain the consequences of shifting priorities if that is a requirement of the task.
- Find out if there are particular ways in which the work needs to be done.

Stage 2 Planning Support
- Establish what support you will need, and ask for it.
- Plan specific times to meet, if necessary.
- Find out what you may need to learn and discuss this with your boss.
- Allocate time, and obtain agreement to this from your boss.

Stage 3 Handling Difficulties
- Deal promptly with difficulties, and consult where necessary.
- Replan the overall schedule and let people know about the change
- Deal with shifting priorities by clarifying them early in the work.
- Reschedule cancelled meetings that may have been arranged to help you.
- Offer some feedback to your manager about the delegation process and suggest ways that you could jointly improve it in the future.

Figure 5.1 on page 33 illustrates the type of issues you should be concerned with if you are receiving delegated work. Work through the list and tick off any of those activities that currently apply when you receive delegated work. As with the earlier exercises, be as truthful as you can and don't worry if some of these ideas are new to you; the 'taking action' section at the end of the chapter will give you some ideas on how to improve.

Taking Action

- Even if you do not handle the initial meeting thoroughly enough with your manager, you can always go back with the questions that have subsequently occurred to you. Do this as promptly as possible.
- Work hard at gaining an accurate and vivid picture of all the issues concerning your ability to complete the task successfully. These may include any or all of the following:
  - timing
  - tangible objectives
  - amount of time to complete the task overall
  - relationship to other bosses
  - an idea of what help you can realistically expect.
- If you are having trouble establishing firm agreements with your manager, explain how important it is for you in order to do the job well.
- Identify those things you will need to learn in order to be able to complete the task, and discuss them with your manager at one of your planning meetings. Make sure that this learning element is taken into account in the overall timing of the work.
- Keep an eye on any problems that you can anticipate, and alert those who need to know about them as quickly as possible.
- If you are uncertain about how your manager will handle any mistakes, raise the topic and establish a route for dealing with them if they happen.
- Stick as rigorously as you can to fulfilling all agreements that you make.
- Keep track of all meetings that you arrange with your manager and if they become difficult to keep to, find some time to alert both of you to the problem. If the problem is becoming critical, approach your boss and explain the possible consequences to the progress of the work.
- Regard yourself as an active participant in the process and contribute accordingly. Where there are problems raise them politely and clearly in a professional way.

Good luck!

Further Reading

We looked long and hard to compile a reading list on the subject of delegation but found the coverage rather disappointing. Many books on management topics have a few lines on delegation but there doesn't seem to be an obvious standard text.

BEE R. and F. *Constructive Feedback*. London, IPD, 1996

COATES J. *Managing Upwards*. London, Gower, 1994

COATES J. *Solving the 126 Commonest Time Problems*. London, JCA, 1988

HANDY C. *Understanding Organisations*. Harmondsworth, Penguin, 1993

GLEESON K. *The Personal Efficiency Program*. New York, Wiley, 1994

LEIGH A. *20 Ways to Manage Better*. 2nd edition London, IPD, 1995

MACKAY I. *Listening Skills*. London, IPD, 1995

PARSLOE E. *The Manager as Coach and Mentor*. London, IPD, 1995

PETTINGER R. *Introduction to Management*. London, Macmillan, 1994

Other titles in the Training Extras series
All titles are £5.95; minimum order three titles.

The Appraisal Discussion
Terry Gillen

The Appraisal Discussion shows you how to make appraisal a productive and motivating experience for all levels of performer – and help your own credibility in the process! Practical advice is given on:

- assessing performance fairly and accurately
- using feedback, including constructive criticism and targeted praise to improve performance
- handling 'difficult' appraisees
- encouraging and supporting reluctant appraisees
- setting, and gaining commitment to, worthwhile objectives
- avoiding common appraiser problems from inadvertent bias to 'appraiser-speak'
- identifying ways to develop appraisees so they add value to the organisation.

1995 48 pages Paperback ISBN 0 85292 618 9

Asking Questions
Ian MacKay

Asking Questions will help you ask the 'right' questions, using the correct form to elicit a useful response. All managers need to hone their questioning skills, whether interviewing, appraising or simply exchanging ideas. This book offers guidance and helpful advice on:

- using various forms of open questions, including probing, simple interrogative, opinion-seeking, hypothetical, extension and precision etc
- encouraging and drawing out speakers through supportive statements and interjections
- establishing specific facts through 'closed' or 'direct' approaches
- avoiding counter-productive questions
- using questions in a training context.

1995 56 pages Paperback ISBN 0 85292 588 3

Businesslike Budgeting
Eric Parsloe and Raymond Wright

Businesslike Budgeting will help you understand what budgets are, why they are important, how to present them – and above all, how you can use them to manage more effectively. It examines in clear, easy language:

- the departmental budget in the company context
- sources of costs and benefits and how to identify those relevant to your proposal
- major types of intangibles and how best to handle them

- presenting and communicating your data
- successfully checking your progress against budget
- assessing and explaining variances.

1995 48 pages Paperback ISBN 0 85292 589 1

Constructive Feedback
Roland and Frances Bee

Constructive feedback plays a vital role in enhancing performance and relationships. The authors help you identify when to give feedback, how best to give it, and how to receive and use feedback yourself. They offer sound, practical advice on:

- distinguishing between 'destructive' and 'constructive' criticism
- using feedback to manage better – as an essential element of coaching, counselling, training and motivating your team
- improving your skills by following the Ten Tools of Giving Constructive Feedback
- dealing with challenging situations and people
- eliciting the *right* feedback to highlight your strengths and opportunities for your own development.

1996 48 pages Paperback ISBN 0 85292 629 4

Customer Care
Frances and Roland Bee

Customer Care will help you understand why caring for your customers is so important; how you can improve the service you offer, and, ultimately, how you can contribute to organisational excellence. Clear, practical guidance is given on how to:

- focus on your customers and the services you provide – both internal and external
- identify your *real* customer needs and how best to meet them
- find out what customers *actually* think of your service or product
- improve communication with your customers – face-to-face, on the telephone or in writing
- turn complaints into opportunities to impress
- monitor, evaluate and continuously improve your customer care.

1995 56 pages Paperback ISBN 0 85292 609 X

The Disciplinary Interview
Alan Fowler

The Disciplinary Interview will ensure you adopt the correct procedures, conduct productive interviews and manage the outcome with confidence. It offers step-by-step guidance on the whole process, including:

- understanding the legal implications
- investigating the facts
- presenting the management case
- probing the employer's case
- diffusing conflict through skilful listening and questioning
- distinguishing between conduct and competence
- weighing up the alternatives – dismissing or dropping the case; disciplining; and improving performance through counselling and training.

1996 56 pages Paperback ISBN 0 85292 635 9

Effective Learning
Alan Mumford

Effective Learning focuses on *how* we learn. It gives invaluable insights into how you can develop your portfolio of skills and knowledge by managing and improving your ability to learn – positively and systematically. Practical exercises and clear guidance are given on:

- recognising the importance of 'achieved' learning
- understanding the learning process – the Learning Cycle and learning style preferences
- taking best advantage of learning opportunities
- creating and implementing a Personal Development Plan
- encouraging and managing a learning culture.

1995 48 pages Paperback ISBN 0 85292 617 0

Listening Skills
Ian MacKay

Listening Skills describes techniques and activities to improve your ability and makes clear why effective listening is such a crucial management skill – and yet so often overlooked or neglected. Clear explanations will help you:

- recognise the inhibitors to listening
- improve your physical attention so you are *seen* to be listening
- listen to what is really being said by analysing and evaluating the message
- ask the right questions so you understand what is *not* being said
- interpret tone of voice and non-verbal signals.

1995 48 pages Paperback ISBN 0 85292 587 5

Making Meetings Work
Patrick Forsyth

Making Meetings Work will maximise your time (both before and during meetings), clarify your aims, improve your own and others' performance, and make the whole process rewarding and productive – never frustrating and futile. The book is full of practical tips and advice on:

- drawing up objectives and setting up realistic agendas
- deciding the 'who, where and when' to meet
- chairing effectively – encouraging discussion, creativity, and sound decision-making
- sharpening your skills of observation, listening, and questioning to get across your points
- dealing with problem participants
- handling the follow-up – turning decisions into action.

1995 48 pages Paperback ISBN 0 85292 637 5

The Manager as Coach and Mentor
Eric Parsloe

A specialist in management coaching, Eric Parsloe describes the principles of coaching and mentoring to enable you to assess and develop your own ability, as well as to improve the performance of others. It includes straightforward guidance on:

- the key skills and appropriate coaching styles
- conducting effective feedback and progress reviews
- establishing your own competence through a series of simple self-assessments
- putting learning theories into practice
- drawing up individual 'learning contracts'
- using mentoring to encourage and support learning
- designing successful development programmes.

1995 48 pages Paperback ISBN 0 85292 586 7

Managing Your Time
Iain Maitland

This book aims to help you prioritise your workload, enabling you to work better, faster and, above all, more effectively. It includes down-to-earth guidance on:

- getting it right first time
- delegating successfully
- recognising time-wasting activities – and people
- tackling paperwork efficiently
- organising work practices and making the best use of travel time
- running meetings better
- handling interruptions and the unwanted telephone call.

1995 56 pages Paperback ISBN 0 85292 584 0

Motivating People
Iain Maitland

Motivating People will help you maximise individual and team skills to achieve personal, departmental and, above all, organisational goals. It provides practical insights on:

- becoming a better leader and co-ordinating winning teams
- identifying, setting and communicating achievable targets
- empowering others through simple job improvement techniques
- encouraging self-development, defining training needs and providing helpful assessment
- ensuring pay and workplace conditions make a positive contribution to satisfaction and commitment.

1995 56 pages Paperback ISBN 0 85292 585 9

Negotiating, Persuading and Influencing
Alan Fowler

Negotiating, Persuading and Influencing will help you develop the critical skills you need to manage your staff effectively, bargain successfully with colleagues or deal tactfully with superiors – thus ensuring that a constructive negotiation process leads to a favourable outcome. Sound advice and practical guidance are given on:

- recognising and using sources of influence
- probing and questioning techniques to discover the other person's viewpoint
- adopting collaborative or problem-solving approaches
- timing your tactics and using adjournments
- conceding and compromising to find common ground
- resisting manipulative ploys
- securing and implementing agreement.

1995 48 pages Paperback ISBN 0 85292 582 4

The Selection Interview
Penny Hackett

The Selection Interview will ensure you choose better people – more efficiently. It provides step-by-step guidance on techniques and procedures from the initial decision to recruit through to the final choice. Helpful advice is included on:

- drawing up job descriptions, employee specifications and assessment plans
- setting up the interview
- using different interview strategies and styles
- improving your questioning and listening skills
- evaluating the evidence to reach the best decision.

1995 48 pages Paperback ISBN 0 85292 583 2

Working in Teams
Alison Hardingham

A highly experienced consultant on teamworking, the author looks at teamworking from the inside. *Working in Teams* will give you invaluable insight into how you can make a more positive and effective contribution – as team member or team leader – to ensure your team works together and achieves together. Clear and

practical guidelines are given on:
- understanding the nature and make-up of teams
- finding out if your team is on track
- overcoming the most common teamworking problems
- recognising your own strengths and weaknesses as a team member
- giving teams the tools, techniques and organisational support they need.

1995 48 pages Paperback ISBN 0 85292 590 5